How to Fail Successfully

How to Fail Successfully

Finding Your Creative Potential Through Mistakes and Challenges

Brandon Stosuy

Abrams Image,
New York

Editor: Samantha Weiner
Freelance Editor: Karrie Witkin
Designers: Kristian Henson
and Jenice Kim
Managing Editor: Glenn
Ramirez
Production Manager: Rachael
Marks

Library of Congress Control
Number: 2021946861

ISBN: 978-1-4197-4654-3
eISBN: 978-1-64700-378-4

Printed and bound in China
10 9 8 7 6 5 4 3 2 1

Abrams Image books are
available at special discounts
when purchased in quantity
for premiums and promotions
as well as fundraising or
educational use. Special
editions can also be created
to specification. For details,
contact specialsales@
abramsbooks.com or the
address below.

Abrams Image® is a registered
trademark of Harry N. Abrams,
Inc.

ABRAMS The Art of Books
195 Broadway, New York, NY 10007
abramsbooks.com

Contents

"I've gotten used to hearing 'no' in various forms throughout my life as an artist and as a person, which means I've tried to form a creative practice and a living practice around building things for myself and others that we've otherwise been denied."

Hanif Abdurraqib
(Poet, writer, curator, author of
They Can't Kill Us Until They Kill Us,
A Fortune for Your Disaster,
and *A Little Devil in America*)

"I love the feeling of entering the unknown. You have to allow yourself a lot of mistakes, and then when you get it right, it's so rewarding."

Björk
(Musician, songwriter,
composer, producer, DJ)*

* Stosuy, Brandon, "Björk on nature and technology," The Creative Independent, September 27, 2016.

"I'm way more scared of never failing than I am of failure itself. If I'm failing it means there's still a lot to learn, and I hope I never stop learning."

Noelia Towers
(Visual artist)

I'm not afraid of failure. If you challenge yourself in your day-to-day life, you're bound to fail, and I'm not interested in simply coasting. I really do like working toward things. As my wife, Jane, said to someone the other day, "Brandon likes to bite off more than he can chew, and then somehow find a way to chew it."

Here's a tangible example of a project that would have failed if I stopped chewing on it: this book. My agent and I had initially pitched a much different idea from what you're now holding. My original plan was to write a more straightforward memoir of sorts, the story of a working-class kid growing up in a small town who discovered punk and found a path to a life he hadn't expected. When my editor and collaborator, Karrie Witkin, read that proposal, she saw another idea within it: Instead of focusing on *what* I'd done, what if we focused on *how* I did it? I was intrigued instead of insulted. And then I thought, because collaboration has always been central to what I do, what if we looked at how my collaborators and friends do what they do, too?

On the surface, this may not sound like failure, but that's only because we kept going. I could have easily said, "No, that wasn't my intention," and taken the book idea somewhere else. The thing is, I'm not sure the original idea was a good one. If I *had* seen the new suggestion as failure, or didn't allow space for collaboration, this book wouldn't exist. Sometimes failure occurs because you force a thing to fail due to ego or shortsightedness. If your first idea doesn't get to the finish line unchanged, is that failure? I don't think so. Making this series has been one of the most rewarding projects of my life.

As it stands, *How to Fail Successfully* is the third volume in a three-part series designed to demystify the creative process and guide people through different aspects of a creative life. The series begins with *Make Time for Creativity* (because carving out time for creative projects is challenging, but fundamental), followed by *Stay Inspired* (which focuses on strategies for generating creative ideas). *How to Fail Successfully*, then, is about how to keep going when you hit various roadblocks.

When I asked Anna Fox Rochinski—one of the musicians I manage—how she characterizes failure in the context of creativity, she responded: "I think micro- and macro-failures are necessary for breakthroughs. The creative process is a series of many small (or big) judgment calls about whether or not to pursue an idea to completion." When you make something new, you start with an idea and submit yourself to a series of unknowns. Different types of failure will assail you at different moments. For that reason, *How to Fail Successfully* is divided into four chapters, each one representing an approach to different expressions of failure: "Failure in Process" (handling self-doubt while making work), "Failure after Launch" (dealing with disappointing results and criticism after the work is released), "Failure, Time, and Timing" (setting priorities based on what you can control), and "Failure and Opportunity" (seeing new possibilities in failure).

Failure is absolutely inevitable in our creative lives (and in life in general); we rarely make gains without mistakes, wrong directions, or any variety of pains. From a young age, we learn to look at what we did *wrong* with a project—the red ink on the school essay—and this lingers longer than any encouraging words we might have received. And when things go right, we tend to erase the mishaps that led to that success. We compartmentalize our successes and failures.

Part of sustaining a creative practice is recasting this kind of thinking and truly learning to see failure as an opportunity; it's inextricable from success. We'll also examine how our ideas of success evolve, which means constantly moving our goal posts to difficult-to-reach places. Writer Hua Hsu provides a poignant example of this: "I think we have professional goals, which often involve just being able to continue doing whatever it is you're doing. And then sometimes we have these more abstract goals: In my case, there's a book I've been working on—or just thinking about, actually—since I was twenty-one. My personal feeling of 'success' is reserved for this thing that's very intimate and as yet unformed, and there have been times when I've felt bummed that 'professionalism' has kept me from doing it. It's a type of failure, insofar as it's failing the principles, impulses, or desires that led me to picking up a pen in the first place."

External validation won't cement your successes or quell your failures. The real work is internal and ongoing.

"Failure is how you learn. It's just a lesson. And if you see it as anything else and project it onto your self-worth, you will crumble. That low self-worth takes up a lotof room in your head. You will give space to jealousy, bitterness, comparing yourself to your peers . . . and that's less room for the creative process to unfold."

Elle Nash
(Writer, critic, author of *Animals Eat Each Other* and *Nudes*, founder of *Witch Craft Magazine*)

The first major lesson, before you go any further into the book, is to look at a setback or deviation in your plan as a pause rather than a failure. Sometimes you need that pause, whether you recognize it or not. It can be a good spot to rest, refuel, and recalibrate so that you can return to your projects from a new (perhaps more exciting) perspective or angle. But before all of that, you need to address what's in your head. Take a moment to jot down any failures that you're carrying with you right now.

Do you have any works-in-progress that you're struggling with at the moment? These could be projects that you can't seem to start or finish, or projects that aren't shaping up as you'd envisioned. Describe them and what is happening (or isn't happening):

_____

_____

_____

_____

_____

_____

_____

Have you launched a finished product into the world and been disappointed by its reception or the results? Write about what happened and how you feel:

_____

_____

_____

_____

_____

_____

_____

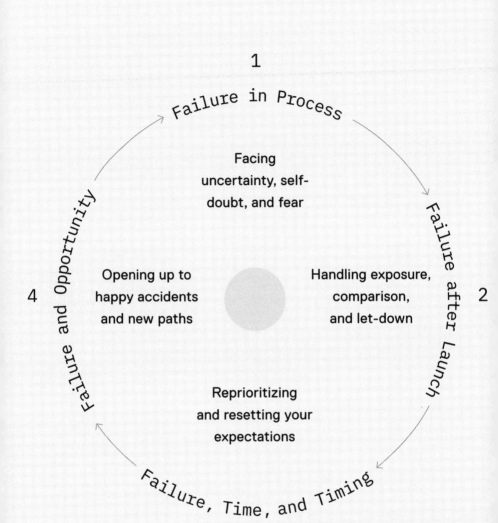

1

Failure in Process

Facing uncertainty, self-doubt, and fear

Failure after Launch

Opening up to happy accidents and new paths

Handling exposure, comparison, and let-down

4

2

Failure and Opportunity

Reprioritizing and resetting your expectations

Failure, Time, and Timing

3

Failure is part of the creative process no matter how long (or frequently) you've been doing what you're doing. Making things never gets easy. Again, this shouldn't be seen as scary or threatening. In a way, it's a comfort. The creative process is a spiral; we constantly return to same issues (and revisit the same failures), but each time, we're armed with more techniques and approaches to make it a little bit easier.

In each chapter, I offer my personal stories of failure while also presenting the advice, observations, and anecdotal experiences of different types of working artists (including musicians, authors, filmmakers, dancers, designers, and visual artists). Purposely, there are a number of different voices here, each helping to suggest the wide variety of ways failure can affect us. As I did with the first two books in the series, I approached friends and people I've collaborated with at one time or another with the aim of making the book feel like a community gathering. These are all people I know, and sometimes we've failed together.

As in the first two books, I also left space for you to jot down your own thoughts and experiences. While reading through— and meditating on—the experiences of all these people, I created prompts to help you draw out your own thoughts and revelations about failure. That's something to remember: You may recognize bits and pieces here or there, or feel some echoes or resonances, but failure is personal, and nobody's experience will be a carbon copy of yours (and shouldn't be).

What's maybe the most important to keep in mind as you read *How to Fail Successfully* is that you're essentially finding ways to keep going when failure does strike. The worst kind of failure is simply stopping. That's the only failure I fear . . . so let's get going.

"My creative process feels to me like piecing together a giant puzzle. Not a standard puzzle. It's more like a gooey, mercurial puddle of phosphorescent pieces that are hot to the touch. The whole thing is uncertain and emotional, and I make sure to luxuriate in it all."

Lydia Ainsworth
(Singer, composer, producer)

We often work alone on projects, and in that solitary space, we can quickly get lost in our own insecurities. One way to begin to move past failure is to give it a personal definition within the context of your creative process: What does it feel like when you fail? How would you describe the emotions you associate with it? The next step is noticing how these emotions shift; failure doesn't have to be an endpoint.

It's helpful to pinpoint where in the creative process you're most vulnerable to blocks or moments of discomfort. This can be tricky: Every creative project is a new situation. You can never recreate the exact experiment more than once, and so it's rare to feel entirely confident in your projects. You tell yourself, "I know I've had success previously, but what if it just doesn't work out this time?" It's also easy to be hypercritical of your work as you're making it.

One way I've been able to push past moments of insecurity is by getting used to them. Once you know these things happen, they don't catch you off guard, and you can find ways to move past them. I've also found it important to identify people who I trust when I'm feeling unsure. There's a huge difference between constructive feedback from a trusted friend and beating yourself up for imagined mistakes. In this chapter, we'll explore these and other ways to get comfortable with being uncomfortable while your creative work is still taking shape.

Creative Management

Making work and moving through creative blocks can be especially hard if you're not being paid for it, or if it's something you're doing purely out of pleasure. In a private situation, when you're pushing along something on your own, it's easy to get stuck inside your head. Essentially, you psych yourself out. It's not uncommon to ask yourself: "Why am I doing this in the first place?" In these non-professional situations, people may argue that the stakes are lower, but that isn't true. Making work is challenging even if you *are* doing it strictly for yourself and don't plan on sharing it with anyone.

But I do think you should share it with someone. I'm often this person. One of the hats I wear is that of an artist manager. I'm there during every part of a musician's process, from when they start working on an idea to when they release it into the world. When one of my artists sends me a demo of a song that they're unsure about, I'm often blown away. I've been moved to tears by songs people thought were subpar. So really, it's usually not the quality of the work that's an issue, it's often a self-imposed block in the mind of the person making it.

A big part of my job is helping people move past these insecurities and frustrations with a work in progress. Records take a long time to put together. There are any number of decisions to be made and potential roadblocks to be faced: Who's the right producer? Who's the right person to mix it? The right person to master the songs once they're mixed? Who's the best collaborator (or collaborators)? The best cover designer? You can second- and third-guess each step, spin out at any time, and never complete the work. It's my job to make sure that doesn't happen.

I do this by diagnosing what's wrong: Does the person need a pep talk? It's worth reminding someone that what they're doing is important. Do they need to get out of their head a bit and see their project in a more objective light? I've suggested many times to take a break from the work and come back to it a few days later with clearer eyes. Is there actually something fundamentally wrong with the project? I'm happy to offer new approaches or angles or collaborators. Is the work actually not as good as it could be? Tough love is part of the job, too.

As much as the creative process is a solitary pursuit, it's not entirely solitary. I think this is the first step toward keeping feelings of failure at bay: Try to think of people in your life who could work as a kind of manager, editor, or sounding board. Learning to share your work with others (or even just one other person) is, in my experience, the most useful way to keep going. I always find a sense of relief when I complete a draft, no matter what shape it's in, and pass it along to someone else.

Finding someone you trust, and who you can show your work to, is a way to retain perspective on what you're doing. The trick, too, is learning to trust yourself.

Labeling the Feeling

When you're making work and find yourself saying, "I'm failing," or "This is a failure," you need to identify the underlying feelings and beliefs precisely. Meg Duffy, a musician I manage, describes the mix of self-judgment and defense mechanisms that pop up when a creative collaboration isn't going well. Annie Bielski, a writer and visual artist, examines the internalized values that hinder her from prioritizing her studio time. Being specific is the first step toward figuring out what kind of support you need.

"If I get the sense of a flow being blocked or disrupted, it can be very alarming emotionally. I can start to feel underprepared, undervalued, and if I'm really following the negative thought pattern train, I can lose the connection between myself and my creative spirit. Thankfully, this happens less and less when I start to be mindful of the language I attach to myself and others, and how I talk about the world in general. Sometimes failure can look like trying to hold onto a song, an approach, a tone, or a lyric that is very clearly not working but feeling too afraid or proud to let it go."

Meg Duffy
(Musician, songwriter,
performs as Hand Habits)

"A practice that has really helped me prioritize [creative] tasks is becoming more aware of how I'm really feeling and examining my underlying beliefs around labor, value, and 'goodness.' I've strangely assigned morality to amoral tasks, like cleaning. I've thought about the hardworking women in my family who don't rest until the floors are clean. Rest comes last. Making my work is not rest, but some days I was treating it as a bonus, the thing that comes last. It's as though my unconscious narrative was, 'If I clean the living room, I am good, and then I have permission to go make a mess in my studio and be bad.'"

Annie Bielski
(Visual artist, writer)

"Lately I've found myself actively trying to move away from the kind of language that oscillates between pass/fail or good/bad or any sort of hierarchical binary when it comes to expressing creativity."

Meg Duffy
(Musician, songwriter,
performs as Hand Habits)

"I have been trying to convince myself that there is no 'failure,' which means ultimately there is no 'right' or 'wrong.' It's not easy, and so, truthfully, I think it has just become a daily ritual where I actually 'fail' and 'breakthrough' multiple times a day."

Indigo Sparke
(Musician, poet, artist)

Any Word but "Failure"

Next time you feel creatively blocked or frustrated with a
piece of work, come back to this page and write down exactly
how you're feeling. Try to avoid judgmental absolutes or
binaries that aren't useful. Do you see any patterns in your
thought process (i.e., one negative feeling or assumption
leading to another)?

Step Back from the Process

Sometimes the feeling of failure is actually a moment when you're frustrated or uncertain about one part of the creative process. Some artists have trouble getting started, others lose momentum in the middle, and getting closure can be the main hurdle for others. Think about which of these general phases represents the most vulnerable stage for you.

"Whenever I'm starting a brand-new thing, a thing I've never made before, it often takes me longer than I can ever anticipate to get into it. I say 'get into it' because for me, the difficulty of getting started happens before the project actually starts. I have to kind of explore my own metaphysical relationship to the project and who I am when I'm making this project. 'Who I am,' meaning what does this project have to do? Where is this taking me that I haven't been before? Why am I doing this? What is the point? Because I have to know that in order to start."

Cat Solen
(Producer, director)

"In my experience, the first part of writing a song is always the least difficult; with any initial idea, there is always a spark and some magic involved. But after this phase, I can reach quite an intense emotional speed bump. I struggle with this idea of putting walls around a song. I think something in me likes the idea of everything being open-ended, with infinite possibilities. So I lament the end of the initial period and always struggle with the middle section."

Aoife Nessa Frances
(Songwriter, musician)

"There are so many times I've overworked something, and with paint, the work is then to keep going and take it to a new place. There's a certain kind of regret that comes with it, and self-deprecation. 'Why haven't I figured out when to stop yet!?' as though there's a formula I'm following. A painting could be good and interesting and complete one hundred times underneath the top layers the audience sees. Hiding things from myself before I destroy them is part of my process."

Annie Bielski
(Visual artist, writer)

Map the Pain Points

When you're working on a project, use this space to make a map of the difficult points in the creative process (i.e. places where the negative self-talk kicks in). You could graph this linearly on an x-y axis (x = degree of pain, y = stage of the process), do a mind map, or write it out.

Five Ways to Address the Inner Critic

How do you remain compassionate toward your own work in progress? How do you stay motivated, incentivize yourself, or hold yourself accountable when a project isn't going well? Here are five strategies to try:

1. Do Now, Judge Later

"I have a few ways of shutting down the failure voice. Mostly I try to give the initial ideas space and time to develop when possible. I try to tell myself that I must 'do now and judge later.' I make short recordings with voice memos on my phone and write ideas for lyrics on scraps of paper, then leave them and come back the next day or in a few weeks. And I'll think, 'Oh, that thing I was really hating yesterday is actually much better than I thought!'"

Aoife Nessa Frances
(Songwriter, musician)

2. Treat Yourself Like a Friend

"Asking myself the questions I try to ask my peers can really bring in a whole world of compassion when I'm hitting a wall or frustration or a creative pothole in a project. Is there a way I'm not looking at the piece that a friend might be able to show me?"

Meg Duffy
(Musician, songwriter, performs as Hand Habits)

3. Shout Down the Critic

"I think it's all about literally standing on a chair and looking in the mirror and being like, 'I fucking believe in myself.' I don't know what it is. I've got no idea—but I know that you have to try and dig deep and find a way of trusting yourself. Prove yourself wrong, prove that you are great."

Holly Blakey
(Artist, choreographer)*

4. Set a Deadline

"I feel like there's nothing more inspiring than a deadline! If I have all the time in the world, I can get washed away by my mind's judgment and doubt. Whereas if I have a strict time limit, there's less time to think and I can get into a flow easier."

Emma Louise
(Musician, artist, writer)

5. Space Out

"Another thing I do is if I'm suddenly feeling a creative block or feeling like I'm totally failing at something, is get a blank piece of paper and a marker and do automatic writing with my left hand (my non-dominant hand). So much good has come from doing this. It shuts down the negative thoughts and allows creativity to flow freely."

Aoife Nessa Frances
(Songwriter, musician)

*Stosuy, Brandon, "Holly Blakey on believing in yourself," The Creative Independent, January 16, 2018.

I find it useful to share with friends. To me, outside eyes and opinions are clarifying. I always frame my project as being a work in progress, which lets the other person know not to see it as finished work. This isn't always easy; it takes time to find the right person, someone you can trust and whose opinion you respect. You have to identify what you need: Is it a pep talk, a thoughtful critique, some technical advice? You probably need different people for all of those things. Working on your own—staying in your own head—can only get you so far:

"One of the things I've learned through failure is that I'm often completely wrong. It's a more valuable lesson than it sounds! I've often found that things are compelling for reasons that the artist does not understand. That doesn't mean you shouldn't have a vision. The vision is the fuel that gets the car moving. Where the car ends up is a whole other matter. Sometimes a vision can be a blind spot. You can miss all the talent and imagination standing at your side. So far, my solution has been to step back at every impasse. To be patient. Rather than immediately scrapping the work and starting over, I'll stop and ask the person I'm working with, 'What do you hear? Is there something worthwhile that has made its way into the work that I'm missing?'"

Geoff Rickly
(Musician, songwriter, writer, singer of Thursday)

Board of Advisors

Jot down the name of the ideal person in your life for the
various kinds of feedback that are valuable in the creative
process:

To reaffirm your value/worth:

To listen to you blow off steam:

To help with a specific technical issue:

To collaborate or explore new ideas:

To offer a valued opinion of the work:

The Puzzle

When we talk about the arc of a creative process, the beginning and end are easy to define, but the middle is the murky space where all of the unknowns unfold. Several artists that I've spoken with liken this phase to solving a puzzle. I think this metaphor helps mitigate the intimidating shapelessness of this middle zone:

"While I'm making the work, I go into major problem-solving mode. Everything becomes a puzzle I need to solve. So even if I start to doubt a certain moment or a part of something, I don't really think, 'This is a failure.' Instead I think, 'OK, this isn't working, this isn't as good as I thought it would be. What can I do right now to make it better?' Even if all I can do is something very insignificant-seeming, I do it! Also, sometimes something early on won't seem right to me, and I sort of have to trust that when I see it in context later it'll make more sense. Sometimes, when combined with the big picture, a little thing that wasn't working before all of a sudden works and fits."

Cat Solen
(Producer, director)

"The surrounding edges of any puzzle are relatively easy to find; they are like the borders of a creative idea I might have for a song. Then comes the trial-and-error stage, which is basically the majority of my process. Overcoming the emotional speed bumps is like playing a game, which can definitely produce bloodcurdling frustration at times, but I never bring myself down about it or ask, 'Why am I doing this?' I like to coast the undulating waves. I catch a glimmer of the puzzle piece at the bottom of the sea buried in the sand, and then I drop it. 'Where did it go??? Ah, there it is. Nope it's gone again. Yes, OK, not what I was thinking . . . but it fits!' If I'm truly stuck, then I will absolutely take a break, step back, and allow perspective to help find the missing piece I'm looking for. This can take five minutes to five years, in my experience."

Lydia Ainsworth
(Singer, composer, producer)

"Of all I do, the part of my job that I continually have the hardest time with is when I have to write a treatment for a music video. Sometimes I have to imagine what the worst music video for this song could be. I've had collaborators who cannot handle this part of the process. For me, though, it helps me really face my fears and understand what it is that I'm afraid of. It helps me come up with absurd and surreal things I wouldn't have thought of before."

Cat Solen
(Producer, director)

"I love hearing songs out in the world and thinking about what I'd do to make them better. On the radio, at CVS, whatever. I truly love stumbling across a bad song out in the wild. It's a fun exercise and helps me approach my own songwriting with a clear head."

Anna Fox Rochinski
(Musician, songwriter, artist)

Invite the Bad Ideas

Here's a counterintuitive way of getting through the painful
early stages of ideation: Welcome and explore terrible ideas.
Why not try it? Think about a project that you're working
on now and brainstorm all of the wrong moves that you make
with it. Or start with something existing that you think is
terrible: What would you do to make it work?

_____

_____

_____

_____

_____

_____

_____

_____

_____

_____

_____

_____

_____

_____

_____

_____

_____

I moved to Canada in my early twenties because I was dating someone who was Canadian. This was before 9/11, when you could show up at the border with a van full of junk (and your cat) and tell them you were going to visit a friend, and they'd let you through. While in Canada, in a town called Lethbridge, I started collaborating with a bunch of artists—painters, filmmakers, sculptors of strange, tiny worlds. I felt like trying to make some visual art of my own.

Something I found intriguing was a short film. A big part of it involved writing. I didn't know how to operate a camera, but I had friends who did, and I thought that maybe they could handle that aspect of it, or they could teach me. With that in mind, I wrote down my idea for a twenty-minute film called *The Kettle,* applied for a first-time filmmaker grant, and waited.

I got the grant. This was both exciting and terrifying. I was definitely a "first-time filmmaker" in that I had never even held a film camera. I remember when I received the letter telling me that the grant was mine, part of me was scared to tell my friends. I figured they'd be excited, but I also wondered if they'd think I was a poseur. Why did I think I deserved this grant money? (I'd honestly kind of hoped I didn't get it so I could just move on and go back to what I was comfortable doing.)

But I did tell them. They *were* excited, we decided to work as a team, and after a couple of months, we completed the project. I have to say that for a large part of it, I suffered from imposter syndrome. The film was based on my script and ideas, and I directed each shot, but I didn't realize I was directing it. I felt like my friends could have made the project without me.

I've heard a similar thing from the artists I manage. They'll say what they think a song should sound like and will suggest a very specific approach to the bass, drum, and guitar, and only later realize, "Oh, hey, I was the producer on that track!"

When I got into graduate school at SUNY Buffalo, the English department didn't need any more teaching assistants, but they did need one in Media Studies. I was offered an Introduction to Video class, and I decided to take it. I spent the summer before heading off to Buffalo teaching myself how to use a video camera. I tried to always stay a few weeks ahead of my students, which I managed to do. Again, I usually felt like an imposter.

The thing is, as I met and became good friends with the other media studies teachers (including my mentor, Tony Conrad), I realized I wasn't faking it and I wasn't an imposter. Sure, I hadn't made a ton of work, but because I had a genuine interest in it and a project I wanted to complete, I was a lot like them. And, in fact, hanging out with these folks led to all kinds of collaborations and my own video projects. Before I knew it, I was making videos constantly and showing them in art spaces, galleries, warehouses, and friends' houses and in my own house, too. We all have to start somewhere, right?

Zone of Proximal Development

Your confidence can suffer from picking projects that either aren't difficult enough or are too challenging. One way to steer yourself away from fears of failure is to identify the next step just outside of your comfort zone. In educational psychology, this is known as the zone of proximal development. It describes the space between what a child can do on their own and what they can do with help from a teacher or parent. In this model, the small failures that a child encounters to gain mastery of something have a big psychological payoff.

I witnessed this when my younger son, Jake, learned how to ice skate. At first, he didn't know how to take a fall, and so he'd hit the ice especially hard and wanted to give up. My wife coached him to crouch a little and widen his base so that he landed more gracefully. Once he accepted that he would fall and knew how to do it better, he was willing to keep practicing. Getting acclimated to fear and failure was necessary for him to take the next step outside his zone of proximal development.

Katie Alice Greer, a songwriter and producer I manage, also strives to work within this zone: "There's a David Bowie quote about how making good art is like wading out into the ocean until you've just reached a place deep enough that you can't quite touch the ground, but you're not so far out that you have to struggle to keep from being carried away. It is now the north star of what I'm always working toward. I do not want to be comfortable. I do not want to drown. I want to stay engaged and to feel challenged by nature."

Chin Above Water

Think about the concept of the zone of proximal development.
What kind of challenges have pushed you, but not too far
(in other words, when a little discomfort yielded a big
result)? Can you translate this to your creative work?

_____

_____

_____

_____

_____

_____

_____

_____

_____

_____

_____

_____

_____

_____

_____

_____

_____

Humiliation Addict

The fastest way to find the edges of your ego (your self-definition) is to do something that makes you really, really uncomfortable. The reward is an expanded sense of self and what you're capable of. Apparently, taking creative risks can become addicting:

"If I'm not a nervous about humiliating myself, I'm probably not doing anything very interesting. Being unsure about something but going for it anyway is so exciting. That mixture of fear and faith is the itch I'm always scratching at. The feeling I get the moment before I do something I've never done before is something I'm always trying to feel again. It ends up feeding itself like any other addiction. Risking humiliation has become the whole point."

Matt Berninger
(Musician, writer, solo artist,
singer of The National)

"Years ago, I realized one of the only reasons I hadn't been able to start a band was because I was afraid of how I'd look as a beginner onstage. When I sat with the logic of this observation long enough, I reasoned that surely, though it'd be tough to put myself in a position to risk utter humiliation, there was no possible way I could literally die from feeling humiliated. So with this certainty in mind, I started looking for any opportunity to face this fear head-on. Sometimes I think I even courted it because of the rush I felt from surviving the terror I associated with public embarrassment. Over time, I have committed to feeling like a beginner at something all the time. Don't get me wrong, it still feels awful sometimes. But I know that I'm not worth any less to myself when I've wandered into unfamiliar territory. In fact, it reminds me of my courage, which makes me feel pretty good."

Katie Alice Greer
(Songwriter, producer, artist)

"There are plenty of wonderful artists I like who stick with the same thing through their whole career. But I thought, what's really exciting is when they start doing something new and it surprises you. . . . I put it down to being of a generation where the people I looked up to—whether they were science people, music people, pop singers, or whatever—were constantly trying new things. Not all the stuff they did was good. I thought, 'Well, that's the way you're supposed to be. That is what's cool.'"

David Byrne
(Multimedia creator,
front person of Talking Heads)*

* Stosuy, Brandon, "David Byrne on not being afraid to fail," The Creative Independent, January 5, 2017.

Risk, Reward

In the left column, make a list of four creative actions that will make you uncomfortable (i.e., performing at an open mic, reaching out to someone you admire, posting your work on social media). In the right column, jot down how you felt after completing each one.

ACTION	RESULT

"My ideas about creativity are very connected to my perspectives of when I used to be a long-distance runner. It's an old running saying that when you feel overwhelmed, just think, 'OK, run one mile and then see how you feel.' In the case of creativity, to begin means you could go deep into something and lose yourself, which is very scary. The mantra, in spite of all of this, should be, 'just do a little something and see what happens.' Undoubtedly, once you're in the thing, you won't want to get out."

Dorothea Lasky
(Poet, professor, author
of *Milk, ROME,* and *Animal*)

What If You Really Hit a Wall in Your Process?

"It's OK to abandon a creative project when the mystery no longer excites me. In this instance, I can see the road the work is directing me to, and either I've been there before and I have nothing new to add this time, or it's simply a dead end that I needed to explore."

Lydia Ainsworth
(Singer, composer, producer)

"I try to operate under the assumption that there are no bad ideas, just ideas that need to be reworked or recontextualized. I kind of hoard material; I have hundreds of demos, song fragments, and voice memos that I refer to often, just in case time and different perspectives can help the stars align."

Taja Cheek
(Musician, curator,
performs as L'Rain)

"I know that if I'm hitting a wall in songwriting, I'll need to start working in a different creative medium altogether. I either paint or sculpt. I find that it brings me back sooner into songwriting with a new, fresh perspective. A palate cleanser!"

Emma Louise
(Musician, artist, writer)

"When something loses the initial inspiration and momentum, I usually feel it loses its original intent and there is no point in forcing something to work. Instead, I focus on what I can accomplish next."

Sasha Grey
(Actor, author, musician, DJ)

Conclusion

"I think that I will feel like a beginner for the rest of my life simply because I am not 'trained.' But that is kind of a gift, too, to always be in a state of wonder and readiness to accept new information. I will never be above learning. I will never arrive, and that is comforting to me."

Sarah Beth Tomberlin
(Musician, songwriter, performs as Tomberlin)

I've never thought of myself as an expert. I honestly can't imagine framing knowledge or a skill in that way. It feels capitalistic. Society has a way of making us think we need to be perfect at things, or authorities, but this really isn't true.

Growing up without much art or obvious "creativity" around me forced me to learn how to do things on my own, and in that way, I've always felt a bit like an imposter because of it. Plus, I do find it exciting is continually try new things, as messy and complicated as those things can be, which also keeps me on my toes. When I was in grad school, it bummed me out to see professors always talking about the "important" paper they'd written thirty years ago, as if nothing they did after it mattered. I don't like to think of life as mastering one thing, then fixating on it forever. The other day, I was talking to an artist on the phone and I said to her, "Growth is stressful." She laughed. Then we both paused and realized, it's true. Growth is stressful, because it puts you into unfamiliar territory. If you never feel uncomfortable, you're also never growing.

I do a lot of projects with my friend Matt. He's mostly known as the singer in the band The National, but he does other stuff, too. I like how he thinks about failure, which is probably why we often end up collaborating. As he said to me, "I'm usually only about 51 percent confident that what I'm doing is going to work. But that 1 percent is enough to bring me back to it. The odds of failure feel very high every time I do anything, so just doing it anyway feels like success."

The thing is, all you really need to keep going is that 1 percent. None of us are ever 100 percent sure about anything, so take whatever percentage of confidence you *do* have, and go from there. Here are some reminders on how to harness it, and how to use it as a catalyst for continuing:

> When the words "I'm failing" surface in your creative process, look for clearer language to express what's happening. Are you frustrated? Impatient? Feeling unprepared? Tired? Do you notice a pattern in how these feelings come up?

> Practice talking back to your internal critic or finding ways to silence it if needed. Show your work in progress to a trusted friend or advisor to get another valid perspective.

> Imposter syndrome is just another version of fearing failure and risking humiliation. It stops you from trying new things when you're worried about losing credibility. Reframe risk-taking as a creative goal. That way, merely trying something is in itself a success.

> You can effectively chip away at fear of failure by identifying the zone of proximal development in your creative process. This is something that feels challenging, but not overwhelming. You'll feel rewarded for your effort and more likely to keep pushing ahead.

"I've gotten wrapped up in the idea that I had to have a ton of public accolades, or x number of people listening to my music in order for it to matter, or to not be a failure. That's a really toxic way to evaluate the merit of your work. The truth is that the most impactful moments for the work will be invisible, private moments that are unquantifiable in their significance."

René Kladzyk
(Musician, songwriter, writer, performs as Ziemba)

It's a scary moment when you release your personal work into the world and hope to find an audience for it. Suddenly it feels like a different project from the one you'd been finalizing behind closed doors. What if people hate it? What if they don't get it? What if nobody responds to it at all? Sharing your creations with strangers will uncover a level of vulnerability and insecurity that you might not have anticipated prerelease. Letdown can take many forms, but you aren't alone.

Many of the people quoted in this chapter are musicians I manage. I work with each of them closely to bring their projects to life and know firsthand that nobody releases anything without a bit of self-doubt. We live in a time where expectations of visibility through social media are high. We get access to results quickly, and the emotional aftermath can start the moment you put something out there. Strangers will have opinions, they'll want to share them, and they have the means of doing so publicly. But in a metrics-obsessed society, it's worth asking ourselves whether attaining these benchmarks of success is really going to benefit us creatively (tip: they mostly won't).

This chapter offers perspectives and strategies for overcoming insecurity, dealing with criticism, facing imposter syndrome, and navigating the comparison traps that arise as you navigate a particular scene or creative field.

Exposed to the World

Think about this: How often have you been proud of something you're making, right up to the point when you're about to share it with someone? So often, "failure" is less about actual failure and more about perceived failure. Perceived or projected failure is tied to self-doubt and not the actual work you're making.

I once moderated a discussion between two musicians, Meg Duffy (aka Hand Habits), who I manage, and Jenn Wasner of Wye Oak and Flock of Dimes, who I don't. Jenn explained to me that she'd made her last Flock of Dimes record in quarantine. She was particularly shut off from others, which was a new space for someone who collaborates often. The record is about the end of a relationship. Because she was recording it alone, she felt free from self-consciousness and embarrassment, and maybe went deeper than she normally would have into her heartbreak, anger, and loss.

Once it came time to share with the label, though, Jenn suddenly felt embarrassed about some of the subject matter. Her first instinct was to tone it down, but she quickly realized there was nothing wrong with the material. It was just that she was no longer experiencing the work alone and she was dealing with internalized misogyny, to an extent. What would people say about the record? Would they find her anger ridiculous? She thought to herself, "My anger is not funny or embarrassing, it's real." She knew this when she made the record, too, but she had that moment of self-doubt when it was about to be heard by other people.

The idea of sharing work can do that; you see what's always been there in a different light. I often tell clients and collaborators that they'll be judging their own work harder than anyone else. I can guarantee that this is true (even in regard to an actual critic reviewing the work with a score to settle). You may be doing a close-up edit of a new video, for instance, and there's a brief moment where a passing shadow bugs you. You fixate on that tiny moment, and it feels like the end of the world. When someone else is watching it, they very likely won't zoom into that one tiny detail, and if they did happen to notice it (they won't), their experience won't be ruined by it.

Sarah Beth Tomberlin, a musician I manage, has identified how to deal with the urge to hold back her work and endlessly perfect it: "The main doubt is probably that it could be better and maybe I should keep working on it. Most creations can always be 'better,' but I'm learning that 'better' might not accurately capture the moment or feeling you are trying to relay. . . . My work is deeply connected to my experience and life, and if that isn't for someone, that is truly OK. It doesn't mean it is a failure." Fear and self-doubt never go away, but we can find ways to move past them.

"It's always been important to me to release things as a time stamp of where I'm at as a producer and creator. I've released CDs out of suitcases in high school, and even though I cringe at them now, it's important to me to share work with people."

Elle Graham
(Musician, songwriter, producer, performs as Woodes)

Ready or Not, Release

Take a moment to write about any self-doubt that comes up when you put your work out there in some way.

_____

_____

_____

_____

_____

_____

_____

_____

_____

_____

_____

_____

_____

_____

_____

_____

_____

Dealing with Disappointment

You've made something, you've put it out there, and then maybe nothing comes of it. Or the attention that it receives is less than positive. How do you get perspective on criticism, lower-than-expected turn-out, or any other disappointments that can come up after releasing your work? Interestingly, the most common response that I've received to that question is to put that project in the rear-view mirror as quickly as possible. There are a few ways to do this:

"[One] thing that helps the blow of an underperforming project, for me, is to already be focusing on what you want to make and do next. Usually by the time something I've made comes out, I'm super deep into something else. I also try to break up with projects when I finish them. I try to not think about them or talk about them for as long as I can . . . a week or a month. That helps me, too."

Cat Solen
(Producer, director)

"I love having a clean slate for a new chapter. I've put everything to do with my first album in a folder and I've filed it away. I have a computer that's just for musicmaking, and I keep it entirely blank except for what I'm working on currently. Between each release, I have tried to make sure I have down time. Following a thread with a friend and going on an adventure or having a late-night conversation or watching a film you've been meaning to watch. I've recognized with time that these things are all part of the process, and there's no guilt attached anymore. On the back of a negative experience with a release, often I just want to dive right back in and create something even better so that I can replace the feelings in my head. It's important to have that space where you are free and giving yourself a clean slate for something new."

Elle Graham
(Musician, songwriter, producer,
performs as Woodes)

Everyone Is a Critic

Something I've told a number of artists I work with: Often a negative review is a failure on the part of the person writing the review! The reviewer misinterprets the work, or it doesn't meet their own expectations for some specific reason, and they focus on that. Same goes for the peanut gallery; you can't force an audience to understand what you do. Instead, it's time for you to be a critic of the critics and decide who's worth listening to and who isn't—especially when the critic is camped out in your head.

"Doubt, for me, is a highly flammable substance that I know how to metabolize into sometimes-great things. I am learning that the doubt articulated by people that I perceive as powerful mirrors my own self-doubt. The fact that it comes from someone that I perceive as larger or more powerful gives me the excuse to prove them wrong. It gives the feeling of punching up rather than self-flagellation. This all sounds super aggressive, but to be honest, this all comes from a deep lack of self-esteem and my constant need to feel like I am doing something valuable."

Matthew Day Jackson
(Visual artist)

"I used to almost compulsively seek out negative reviews, mean tweets, stuff like that. Eventually I realized [what] I was really seeking: a sense of feedback, a response to whatever my work is shouting into the void. A little insecurity might be whispering, 'It's not very good,' while I'm working, but if I can find a real person to give the insecurity a voice, I have someone to play a kind of mental chess with. Realizing that this is not really about anybody else's interpretation of what I'm doing and simply me squaring off with myself, has been a hugely helpful realization. Having this formidable opponent is what encourages my supportive feelings about what I'm doing to get stronger. If I have the potential for a very strong inner critic, I have just as much potential for a very strong internal fanbase."

Katie Alice Greer
(Songwriter, producer, artist)

How Do You Handle a Bad Review?

"If I get a bad review, I have a few things I like to do. Number one, I think of my favorite movie, *The Big Lebowski*, and quote the Dude to myself out loud: 'That's just, like, your opinion, man.'"

Lydia Ainsworth
(Singer, composer, producer)

"One critic noted that I was overly wordy and never let the band play a note of music without choking everything off with more lyrics. At the time, it showed me a flaw I hadn't seen, and I hated that record for the next two years of touring on it. Now I think it gives the record a claustrophobic feeling that mirrored the time period perfectly."

Geoff Rickly
(Musician, songwriter, writer,
vocalist of Thursday)

"It's easy to confuse the most hurtful feedback for the most honest, because it is usually much more specific than, 'Hey man, great set.' Seeking out negative feedback is another way of working through my own doubts about my work."

Katie Alice Greer
(Songwriter, producer, artist)

"Is it lying to yourself if you tell yourself that the project's biggest fans just haven't found it yet? I do that a lot."

Cat Solen
(Producer, director)

"Insecurity is usually more of a sprinter and eventually gets exhausted, whereas self-compassion is more of a long-distance thing for me, and fortunately, those are the only races with myself that I am trying to win."

Katie Alice Greer
(Songwriter, producer, artist)

"I've never experienced acute imposter syndrome where I suddenly feel like I'm somewhere I don't belong. It's more of a general feeling that I never belong anywhere. No matter where I am or what I'm doing, I think I'm always a little anxious to get out and move on before anyone finds out I have no idea what I'm doing."

Matt Berninger
(Musician, writer, solo artist,
singer of The National)

We've all felt imposter syndrome. The sort of self-doubt that has to do with feeling you're not on par with others and not deserving success or recognition. Imposter syndrome can surface when you're starting something new, but you can feel it, too, among peers who are more well-known or "successful" to different degrees than you.

One sort of "failure" involves people fearing someone is only paying attention to their project because of someone else associated with it. I often hear things like, "Folks are only coming to this group art show because of the other painters in it," or, "They hired me for this project because they know I'm friends with so-and-so." I point out that even if that *is* the hook that gets someone to pay attention at first, people won't continue to engage with your project just because of who you know. Also, viewing your output through this lens is limiting. It comes down to you as an artist deciding for someone else why they like what you're doing. Frankly, that's not up to you.

One way to push away thoughts of imposter syndrome is to shift focus; instead of looking at abstract metrics and projections, highlight the areas of genuine engagement. Genuine engagement is powerful, and even small examples of it can keep you going. It doesn't need to be a room full of screaming fans. Or a bestseller. I still remember when my fourth-grade teacher told me that she liked my writing. That stuck with me and made me think, "Maybe I'm a writer?" It was a simple comment, but it nudged me onto a path. It was inspiring!

I run The Creative Independent largely on my own. I look at the analytics each day, and I see how traffic is doing or that people are reading one story more than another—but it still feels so abstract. It's a measure, but it's a distant one. For me, it's the notes, emails, and Instagram comments from readers telling me how much the site means to them that keeps me going. I make my work for people, not for numbers or some idea of what it means to have "made it." Mainstream society's notions of what it means to be successful are pretty boring. I don't need awards. When I see those emails (even if they're just a sentence), I smile, feel a rush of adrenaline, and all the effort feels worth it.

For me, it's not about winners or losers, it's about human connection. A few people who respect your work matter. Find those people and moments of acknowledgment and hold onto them. You don't need to convince the entire world to embrace your work. Doubt and feelings of imposter syndrome disappear, but the work remains, so make it.

"My wish is for my music to be a friend to someone in need, a companion like it was to me when writing. If my music helps even one person, I can't think of anything better than that."

Lydia Ainsworth
(Singer, composer, producer)

Keep a Compliments List

It's incredible knowing your work has meant something to
someone else, even just a single person. That sort of
affirmation, no matter how small, can wash away self-doubt.
One of the artists that I manage covered a song, and I shared
it with the original artist. He wrote back a brief, kind
note, something that she'll always remember. Think about
moments of engagement like this in your own life and make a
list of them here.

Comparing "Success Stats"

Each year the streaming platform Spotify disseminates "Spotify Wrapped," a promotional campaign that displays what users have streamed the most throughout the year. If you're an artist, you can access information about how your songs did on the platform: How many people streamed a song? How much did your reach grow since last year? Are you big in Russia? The analytics are legitimately interesting, but they also contribute to feelings of inadequacy and failure. Artists post these on their social media, where other artists see them and can't help but compare themselves.

In independent music, 2020 was the year of Phoebe Bridgers. She started 2020 as a respected (but not super famous) indie musician and ended with four Grammy nominations and a huge following. Because she's a legitimate peer of so many independent artists, and not a distant major-label pop creation, it's easy for other independent artists to look at her stats and say, "Phoebe Bridgers got so many more streams than me. Am I a failure?"

When you do this, you fall into the comparison trap. You look at the awards and rankings without thinking, "Wait, Phoebe Bridgers has been around for years, and this just happened to be the year she took off." Stats simplify. They erase setbacks and failure and place hard work in the shadows, offering a highlight reel of successes.

Escaping the comparison trap is also about getting out of a scarcity mindset when it comes to ideas. We block ourselves with a fear that our ideas aren't good enough, aren't original, and won't measure up to what's "out there." It's easy to latch on to similarities between your work and the work of your peers and worry that people will assume you're deliberately copying.

When we're highly self-critical and narrow our field of vision by comparing ourselves to just a few other artists, we're being extremely ungenerous to our creativity.

Looking at your work side-by-side with what other artists are doing and assuming that the whole world will draw the exact comparisons is a kind of tunnel vision. I know that it's easy to lose perspective when you are deep in a project, but when you focus too much on other people, you're missing out on ideas that have fallen through the cracks. You need to take a step back and broaden what you see, because honestly, ideas, and the way you can combine them, are endless.

I'd also suggest recognizing when you've put a new spin on something that's been done before. It's common for shared imagery or the same general concept to pop up, but it's the smaller graphic design decisions and unique human particulars that make each project different. For instance, think about the hundreds (and hundreds) of human skulls that have appeared on metal, goth, and punk albums. No two are exactly alike—unless, pardon the pun—it's an intentional nod.

It's human nature to compare. Even though there are people doing better and people doing worse than us, we focus on those doing better and assume because we aren't "doing as well," we're failures. It's essential to keep in mind that no two paths are the same and there really are no overnight successes. Stop now and then, pull back the curtain, and ask people how they got where they are. Switch out comparison for community, collaboration, and empathy. Remember that only you can make the work you're making.

"I think I thought less about failure before I started releasing music, as often the 'releasing' and promotion of art is the part that can have specific numbers and information attached that can pull me into thinking about not getting the outcome I'd hoped for. It's refreshing hanging out with friends outside of the music bubble who aren't aware of those numbers or strategies. As I zoom out wider from my process, I realize that everything is quite insular, and from the outside, it's fine!"

Elle Graham
(Musician, songwriter, producer, performs as Woodes)

Immeasurable Victories

Think about success in ways that aren't defined by awards or stats. How do you feel when you get up early to work on a creative project before anything else can distract you? What's it like to share progress with a friend and feel proud to do so? These accomplishments are essential to the creative process—even if they're small, idiosyncratic, and too personal to post on social media—because they help you wake up each day and keep going. What are your immeasurable victories?

Escaping the Comparison Trap

Failure can take the form of being overwhelmed by the competition—the idea that there are so many people just like you, doing what you want to do, and maybe doing it better. It's important to recognize when you're using other people as a measuring stick. It's inherently self-limiting. Here are some more useful ways to handle a very human tendency to compare:

"I can do this thing where I'm watching a show, and just because of the place we live in and the scenes we run in and our ages, I'll suddenly be like, 'Oh my god, this person is doing the *exact* same thing that I feel like I'm writing right now!' Even though somebody else would look at those two projects and feel like they are not related on any level. If you're self-obsessed enough, you'll somehow just decide that everything everyone else is making is the same as what you're doing. When I feel that way, I'm like, 'Nope, I'm not going to see any shows.' It's hard for me sometimes, but I also feel like I need and want to support my friends whose work I'm really invested in. So this is something that I have to get over all the time. Still, it's easier for me to see music or go to a poetry reading or something. I don't feel competitive with it because it's too different."

Erin Markey

(Comedian, performance artist, singer)*

*Rachel, T. Cole, "Erin Markey on trusting yourself," The Creative Independent, February 16, 2018.

"When I was a teenager, a new kid moved to town and a lot of people said we looked so much alike we could be twins. I didn't think we had that much in common, but it didn't stop me from beginning to draw comparisons between us. Charlotte got better grades; was she smarter than me? Did people call me the uglier version of Charlotte behind my back? Eventually I graduated, and how I measured up to Charlotte didn't matter anymore, because nobody in college knew who she was. When I realized that this pointlessly cruel battle was actually my own feelings of inadequacy challenging me to an arm wrestle, I vowed to not let it get the better of me again. So now if I'm comparing myself to somebody else, I try to see if I can decipher what part of me is trying to arm wrestle another. I try to figure out where I haven't been showing myself enough compassion or appreciation and give myself more."

Katie Alice Greer
(Songwriter, producer, artist)

No Comparison

"Competition can make things feel fun," says Katie Alice
Greer, "but any time the game feels like I'm competing
with someone besides myself, the fun gets poisoned. It also
distracts me from the blueprints in my head for what I'm
trying to make." Take a moment to reflect on a time when you
fixated on comparing yourself to someone else. What were you
missing or undervaluing about yourself in that process?

_____

_____

_____

_____

_____

_____

_____

_____

_____

_____

_____

_____

_____

Conclusion

"I used to take everything personally: a bad performance, a low turnout at a show, a bad record review. But every time I've failed at something so badly that I feel bumped off the track I was heading down, I end up learning so much about myself and taking an inventory of what is really important to me. Plus, if being 'successful' was the only thing that kept me going, I would have quit making art many years ago! And that would have been a big mistake for me."

Felix Walworth
(Musician, producer, photographer, performs as Told Slant)

I feal very much aligned with Felix Walworth's thinking; I make work because it makes me happy. The "fame" side of things has never mattered to me. Our work matters even if it doesn't have the reach or recognition that we hoped to get for it. Even criticism and negative reviews are at their core a form of encouragement. "I think part of the reason I was ever drawn to criticism is because I was very bad at making things—songs, movies, drawings—but I wanted to stay adjacent to the creative world as long as I could," says writer Hua Hsu. "People who can write songs or come up with melodies or paint or whatever possess magic. I admire anyone who can do that." Criticism exists to be in conversation with the work.

Nevertheless, it's healthy to cultivate some detachment from how your work is received. "Even though I want to be accountable to my work, I have to remember that the work is only one form of an extension of me," says Sarah Beth Tomberlin. "Letting go of the fear of criticism leads to freedom to keep discovering joy in experimentation, happy accidents, collaboration, and even the fear of taking a break. We grow from criticisms, even if only learning how to control our need to feel understood, because I don't think anyone or any work can be perfectly understood. So let it go."

It's essential to stop and think about what it is you want and to figure out why it is you make what you make. It's different for each person. What will make you happiest? The most fulfilled? What is it that you really hope to attain from your creative work? Focus on that and try to keep these things in mind throughout the life of your project:

> Feeling exposed when you're releasing something personal into the world is to be expected, but don't second-guess the work itself. Look at it as a time stamp of where you are now, creatively.
> Keep making stuff as you release projects; don't wait for critical reception for permission to make your next move.
> Criticism is not created equally. Separate the negative reviews that come from people who simply don't understand your work from the constructive feedback that dovetails with your own thoughts about what might be underdeveloped in your project.
> Comparing yourself against other people's success is natural, but it's ultimately myopic, self-limiting, and unhelpful when it comes to seeing the unique contributions that you could be making. Why choose a few artists as the benchmark when you can be charting your own course?

"We don't have to carry our failures into tomorrow or even the next hour. Something that has stuck with me is the idea that we cannot waste time in advance; as Arnold Bennett wrote, 'You can turn over a new leaf every hour if you choose.'"

Madeleine Dore
(Writer, interviewer, speaker, founder
of Extraordinary Routines)

"The turtle wins the race, or at least stays in it."

Josh Fadem
(Actor, comedian, *30 Rock,
Better Call Saul, Twin Peaks*)*

*Stosuy, Brandon. "Josh Fadem on putting in the time," The Creative Independent, June 27, 2017.

It's easy to blame our "failures" on not having enough time or having bad timing. The thing is, we all have twenty-four hours a day. The trick is to be clear about giving priority to creative projects while also accepting that sometimes there just isn't time to finish the work we're envisioning. This why we do need to take the long view and to find ways to keep going. Our creative ideas need time to ripen.

Over the years, I've had a number of mentors who were much older than me. Part of what I found inspiring about them was that they managed to be productive on their own terms, continue evolving, and leave a mark. One of these mentors, Tony Conrad, had gone to Harvard to study math and got his degree in mathematics, but ended up being best known as a pioneering minimalist composer, experimental filmmaker, and visual artist. He followed one inspiration to the next, learned in real time, and kept moving. He took his time seriously.

In this chapter, we'll look at how time relates to all of our creative work. We need boundaries to protect our creative space and deadlines to incentivize us, but we also need to let go of the idea that "success" must occur within a specific timeframe in order to justify continuing a creative pursuit. I would argue it's exactly the opposite.

Shifting Priorities

When I was a teenager, I found my path to creativity via punk rock, and so I gravitated toward playing music. I took guitar lessons with a guy a couple of towns over. I'd bring him three-chord punk songs and ask him how to play them; he almost seemed insulted. I practiced, and I was decent, but I didn't excel.

For a long time, I was happy to play in bands with friends who were more talented than me. I'd be the rhythm guitarist, and I was good at coming up with song titles and the designs for our demos and releases, so I played a part. I was in a bunch of bands from my teenage years, through college, and even in graduate school. I wouldn't give any of that back—we toured the country in a van, we met incredible people and slept on disgusting floors, I got to have the feeling of watching people dance and sing along. It was great. It was a big part of my identity.

Back in graduate school, I was talking to my friend Ben about something I was writing at the time—probably a record review, or a piece for my zine—and he casually said something like, "You know, you're a great writer and an OK musician. Do you ever think maybe you should dedicate more time to just writing?"

Ben's comment stopped me in my tracks. It made me pause and consider how much time I was dedicating to a band that played a lot of shows, toured, and had a lot of practices. The fact that I couldn't imagine putting any more time into it, but that I could imagine writing endlessly for hours, and that this idea made me happy, gave me the courage to admit that I was burnt out on that group.

It was a painful realization, but it was also freeing. It felt like a load lifted. You can't spend all your time doing things you're just OK at if you want to get anywhere with the things you're good at. I realized I needed to prioritize and that I'd just needed someone to tell me, "Go write. Make time for what you love." So I put my energy there.

When I quit the band, it didn't mean that I completely stopped making music. I formed a noise group with some friends, and we would meet in an attic once a week, play for a couple of hours, and that was it. I enjoyed the process, and it was fun to be part of this collaboration, but it gave me time to pursue the things I was more interested in doing. And, for me, it worked: Shortly after graduate school, I ended up publishing my first book, *Up Is Up, But So Is Down*.

Focusing on writing over making music wasn't the complete sacrifice it may have seemed like at first. I wrote about music for years at Pitchfork. I've curated a number of music-related art events, continue to book shows, and most exciting to me, I manage a number of musicians and help them in all aspects of their careers. I listen to demos, suggest producers, and collaborate on artwork.

In fact, years ago, that band I'd quit was asked to reunite for a single show. When I told this to Jane, my wife, who was my girlfriend at the time, she said: "You can play music?" It was a shock to her because I'd fully committed to writing and curating by then. I did go back and play that show in Buffalo (and still remembered how to play the songs).

"Often it's just easier to say yes to everything because then you don't have to deal with the feelings that come with saying no to something or the fear of missing out. Or the fear of burning a bridge or hurting somebody's feelings. It keeps you constantly busy, so you don't have time to think about anything else."

Erin Markey

(Comedian, performance artist, singer)*

*Rachel, T. Cole, "Erin Markey on trusting yourself," The Creative Independent, February 16, 2018.

When I spoke with the punk-rock icon, actor, and podcaster Henry Rollins once, he told me that he had a habit of always saying yes. He figured if he was terrible at something, there was no harm in being terrible that one time. He also has a hard time sitting still: "I just say yes a lot. That's how I've ended up in, like, thirty movies and a bunch of TV. I've never taken acting lessons. I just want to do stuff." He added, "I'm not a tough guy. I'm not brave. I'm just curious. I'm very well aware of how quickly life goes."**

He joked that this "just do it" approach contrasted greatly with his childhood friend, Ian MacKaye, another punk legend, who is known for being especially selective. MacKaye's method comes from a kind of ethical standpoint where he only wants to do things that measure up to a specific set of ideals. In fact, when I interviewed him once in front of a live audience, he said plainly, "I say no a lot," and the audience erupted in laughter. No matter the major differences in philosophy (yes always vs. no most of the time), they're two of the most prolific and long-standing figures in their field. It's because they each found what worked best for them.

Saying yes to too many things can leave you with no time to do any of it. It can be how we avoid taking a hard look at our priorities and letting external factors dictate what we produce. Then again, saying yes is how we challenge ourselves and push ourselves into new places. Think about where you fall on the yes/no spectrum, and whether you need to adjust your approach to position yourself for creative growth.

**Stosuy, Brandon. "Henry Rollins on defining success," The Creative Independent, March 27, 2017.

"I'm horrible at saying no. I don't like it! But I'm figuring out that if I don't say no with words, a no will emerge through circumstance: not meeting deadlines or not making work I'm proud of."

Taja Cheek
(Songwriter, musician, curator, performs as L'Rain)

"I've gone through phases where I've said yes to everything as an exercise to either get experience, get money, keep busy, meet people. Then I've gone through phases where I've said no to everything because it became exhausting with little reward, and I want to focus on my own stuff."

Josh Fadem
(Actor, comedian, *30 Rock*, *Better Call Saul*, *Twin Peaks*)

"I work at boundaries all the time, and it can feel awkward. A really helpful tool for me is remembering that I can take a moment before responding or committing to something. Something as simple as, 'I will think about this and get back to you,' has saved me a lot of stress."

Annie Bielski
(Visual artist, writer)

"While my instinct is to say yes to opportunities I used to covet, I'm only taking on projects that enrich me creatively and spiritually. I've learned that being a human is more important than producing work for the sake of a byline."

Marcus J. Moore
(Writer, author of *The Butterfly Effect: How Kendrick Lamar Ignited the Soul of Black America*)

"I've always been great at showing up for others, but not for myself. Now that I am acutely aware of this, I feel more motivated and energetic about my own personal long-term goals. By setting boundaries and understanding my worth, I have prevented myself from saying yes to people that were trying to use me for their own gain."

Sasha Grey
(Actor, author, musician, DJ)

Positive Rejection

Write a letter to one activity or opportunity (it could be a hypothetical one) that you'll need to turn down in order to focus on a creative project that really matters. Emphasize why saying no is difficult and how important it is to you to pursue this project right now.

Failure, Time, and Timing

It Comes Down to Timing

When I first decided to give it a go as a freelance music writer, I gathered together a bunch of writing clips and mailed—not emailed—them out to a bunch of editors. I didn't get a single response.

When I mentioned how discouraged I was, a friend pointed out that the timing and approach of my outreach was terrible. I did it toward the end of the year, when people were all focused on their year-end coverage and at the end of their annual budgets. My friend suggested that I wait until the spring, draft short introductory *emails*, and provide links to a few carefully selected pieces that way.

I followed this advice, heard back from a number of editors, and within a very short time was writing regularly about books and music for the *Village Voice*, *Time Out New York*, *Spin*, and others. I also ended up with a regular writing role at Pitchfork that led to a full-time job. One of my tasks there was sorting through the pitches of other people just starting out. I did this for many years.

From an inside perspective, I can tell you that often the road to acceptance or rejection is out of your hands. Did the editor approve one too many pieces this week? Did someone else pitch a similar piece an hour ago? Did the editor happen to have too many emails the day you wrote and just honestly miss your pitch? How could you know?

I didn't know any of this when I was the one making the pitches. If I'd seen my own first effort as a failure and hadn't tried again, I wouldn't have gotten that Pitchfork job, and I wouldn't be writing this book. If you've been rejected, try another approach. Follow up tastefully. If one outlet passes, try another. It's essential to be adaptable, humble, and to keep trying.

Try Again

Think about a rejection that you've received, or some form
of outreach that you did regarding your work that didn't get
a response. What if you gave it another try? Jot down some
ideas about what you'd do differently this time.

Out of Time

Failure can come about when you're striving to meet an arbitrary finishing point (aka a deadline). While some people feel that they work best under pressure, realistically, it's difficult to churn out consistently satisfying work on the clock. Maybe the trick is to think of time as a container and scale your expectations to fit it; your project might not be the best it could be, but at least it exists, and others may not be as critical of it as you are.

"I've applied to so many calls for art with an extremely short deadline, and even though I usually make it on time, sometimes the results can be a bit of a disaster or simply something I am not proud to show. I keep telling myself that deadlines are the devil (most of them!) but without them, I wouldn't be able to know my limitations, to know how far I can push myself."

Noelia Towers
(Visual artist)

"Deadlines don't necessarily mean that the project or song has to be completely finished. I find that when I'm rushing for a deadline, I don't have time to really criticize myself, and I often come up with the most interesting lyrics, melodies, or songs. If I don't have a deadline, I can get really lost. Or I just won't finish things. Having trusted friends or people I work with that I can show my work to is so important. Even just the act of sharing or being excited to share something with someone can be a form of a deadline."

Aoife Nessa Frances
(Songwriter, musician)

"I've had situations where I didn't give myself enough time and was happy with the result. Conversely, I've also procrastinated and blown it. But I can't completely condemn procrastination. It's case by case. I pick the perspective I'm going to have that seems to suit me best in the moment:

'Here I'm going to not care and just show up and trust that I'm enough.'

'This time I'm going to overprepare and be so polished I'll be ready for anything!'

'This time I'm going to not care and be so sloppy that I'll be ready for anything!'

'The universe will know I had no time and forgive me if it's bad.'

'The universe is watching; I better be the best.'

'The universe is never watching and doesn't care; it doesn't matter how I do, just have fun.'

Other times, as I've gotten older, I've thought, 'I don't think I need to emotionally drain myself for this, I've been preparing with experience for twenty years, I'll be fine.'"

Josh Fadem
(Actor, comedian, *30 Rock*,
Better Call Saul, *Twin Peaks*)

Deadlines

What's your relationship to deadlines? Would setting personal
deadlines help your creative project, or would it deter? Read
through Josh Fadem's various approaches to deadlines on the
opposite page, and jot down any that seem like good advice
for you right now.

Putting in the Time

When you work at something slowly and surely over time, you often get better at that thing. You also create a larger body of work to pull from. Think about these quotes from author Jason Reynolds and musician Phoebe Bridgers, and how the combination of putting in the work and creating a larger depository of unused lines helps them with their current projects. It's worth noting, too, that Reynolds put out five books before he made the *New York Times* Best Seller list, and Bridgers wasn't nominated for a Grammy until she'd been releasing music professionally for six years. Overnight success is rare.

> "You make things, and then you let them germinate. I think that's sort of my rule. It's not always about termination; sometimes it's about germination. Let them sit and germinate. Let them grow. Let them take root. Let them figure out who it is that they are. And then you can go back and tap into them later on and say, 'Ah, this is what I made you for . . .'"

Jason Reynolds
(Author of the *New York Times* best-selling Track series and National Book Award finalist for *Ghost*)*

*Stosuy, Brandon, "Writer Jason Reynolds on being human in your work," The Creative Independent, December 13, 2018

"I have lines from when I was a teenager that I still haven't found a way to use, and it's a great feeling when you finally find a way. But a lot of time they're an aside. They're throwaway lines that helped get the song started. I think that's just from getting better at writing and not just clinging to, 'I had that one idea, now I have to use it.' But every once in a while, the magical feeling happens where you're writing something and then you're like, 'Oh, maybe this is finally the opportunity to use that one thing, or one line.'"

Phoebe Bridgers
(Songwriter, musician, Grammy nominee for Best New Artist in 2020)**

**Stosuy, Brandon, "Matt Berninger and Phoebe Bridgers on how they write what they write," The Creative Independent, July 28, 2020

"I'd have to say that a lot of my earlier work feels like it's a failure to me, because I can go back and see the places where I've made mistakes or where my work is just too sophomoric. However, I often have people say how much they like it, because the work reflects a rawness and a lack of concern for what the audience thinks. It was a lot more free than my work is now. And in some ways, that is its own kind of success."

Elle Nash
(Writer, critic, author of
Animals Eat Each Other and *Nudes*,
founder of *Witch Craft Magazine*)

Revisionist History

Set aside some time to revisit an early example of your
writing, an old sketchbook, a rough recording, or any
material from your creative archive. Is there a seed of a
new idea germinating there? An approach, or a lack of self-
consciousness, that you want to recapture? Reflect on the
merits of your old work here:

_____

_____

_____

_____

_____

_____

_____

_____

_____

_____

_____

_____

_____

_____

_____

_____

_____

The Long View

You may have the right idea at a time that feels right to you, but when you put it out into the world nothing happens. "Wait, was it the wrong idea, after all?" Not necessarily.

Maybe it was the right idea surfacing at the wrong time. The thing I try to keep in mind is that we don't get just one chance, and we don't need to succeed in *just one day*. Things take time, and it'll serve you best to consider the long view. The work you make exists and is available for rediscovery in the future, and success can happen at any time in the life of a creative work.

When the COVID-19 pandemic began, people had to cancel the tours that would have helped them support their records. Most artists were worried about this, but the extra time gave them space to reflect on the ways that touring could be improved in the future. Importantly, it also gave them more time to take better care of themselves, to spend more time on their art, and to rest at home.

As a result, many of the artists I manage completed new records, signed new record deals, found publishing deals, and are arguably better off now than they would have been if touring *had* been possible. And, for people who'd released music right as COVID-19 started and were stressed about not being able to tour, their music is now being rediscovered.

Creative work doesn't exist in a vacuum. Although one project may not land the way you wanted it to when it first came out, if you keep going, people are bound to go back and see what you've done previously, and momentum can pick up in that way. There's a reason for reissues, reunion tours, and returns.

Things don't have just one chance to succeed.

I've experienced this in my own work. In 2003, during the early days of Pitchfork, I reviewed the Sufjan Stevens album *Greetings from Michigan: The Great Lake State*. It ran on the site with a positive score, but not with the coveted Best New Music label attached to it. Sufjan had released two studio albums prior to *Michigan* but was still relatively unknown at the time. The founder of Pitchfork, my friend Ryan, read my review when it ran, listened to the record, and loved it. He decided to rerun the same review, this time with an even higher 8.5 score and, yes, Best New Music. To this day, many people point to that review for pushing Sufjan to a bigger audience and the successful career he has now.

Also a couple of years ago, Tom Hanks tweeted about the comedian and actor Aparna Nancherla; suddenly more people knew who she was and checked out her work. As she put it when I asked her about that moment, "You can't plan it or map it out exactly. You have to be a little adaptable. When stuff like the Tom Hanks thing happens, it's so cool and unexpected. I guess it bolsters the fact that you're like, 'Oh, I'm doing the right things,' or 'I'm getting out there in the way I want to be,' . . . [but] the part that's in my control is only *my* part of it."* Once you do *your* part and create the work and put it out into the world, you never know when it may get a retweet or a cosign or find an audience. Every retweet, all said, is a second chance!

*Stosuy, Brandon, "Aparna Nancherla on being more than just funny," The Creative Independent, January 4, 2017.

"You don't expect things to happen. You don't think, 'OK, in a year's time, it's going to be this huge emblem.' I try not to presume that. It's more like I'm grateful for every step of the way."

Björk
(Musician, songwriter, composer, producer, DJ)*

*Stosuy, Brandon, "Björk on creativity as an ongoing experiment," The Creative Independent, December 14, 2017.

Failure, Time, and Timing

An Ongoing Experiment

The idea of failure seems less daunting when you consider it in the context of Björk's thoughts on removing expectations, taking on an expansive view of time, and allowing creativity to be an ongoing experiment. In her process, a project never really ends, so there isn't a fixed point at which it can be judged a failure. There's always the possibility of taking the work one step further:

"I guess it's a lot about timing. If there isn't the next step and it doesn't feel right, there will definitely be times where I don't do it. But in my mind, I don't look at it that way. It's more like maybe it could happen in ten years' time. Maybe it could happen in fifty years' time. That's the next step. Or somebody else will look at it and it will inspire them to write a poem. I look at it more like that, like it's something that I don't own. The minute your expectations harden or crystallize, you jinx it. I'm not saying I can always do this, but if I can stay more in the moment and be grateful for every step of the way, then because I'm not expecting anything, nothing was ever abandoned. . . .

I like things when they're not completely finished. . . . There were at least one or two albums [where] we made all the songs too perfect, and then we overcooked it in the studio, and then we go and play them live and they're kind of dead. I think there's something in me, like an instinct, that doesn't want the final, cooked version on the album. I want to leave ends open, which is probably why I end up still having people do remixes, and when I play them live, I feel different and the songs can grow. . . .

Don't hold your breath for five or seven years and not release anything. Then you've just got clogged up with way too much stuff. Maybe you've gained some immaculate, perfect versions of some of the songs, but overall, I think there's more minus to that because of how you clog your own flow. You lose contact to the part of you, your subconscious, that's writing songs all the time, and the part of you that's showing it to the world. As much similarity between those two parts of you, I think, the better. That's more important, to sustain that flow, than to wait until things are perfect. . . .

When you release an album, it's important to keep the flow going, and if you have anything extra or new, you use it as fuel for your next thing. . . . It's an experiment that keeps going."*

*Stosuy, Brandon,"Björk on creativity as an ongoing experiment," The Creative Independent, December 14, 2017.

Failure, Time, and Timing

Take a moment to reflect on the many points that Björk
raises about the duration of a creative process. What feels
applicable to you and the current stage in your creative
experiment? Are you being too perfectionistic before putting
yourself out there? Are you too focused on specific outcomes
and expectations for the work? Does it help to just identify
the next step?

_____

_____

_____

_____

_____

_____

_____

_____

_____

_____

_____

_____

_____

Conclusion

"Ideas don't have expiration dates."

Brandon Breaux

(Visual artist, designer)*

I owe a lot of my thoughts in this chapter to my friend Kenny Doren, who was an incredible video artist based in Calgary, Alberta, Canada. At one point, he was visiting me in New York City, and we'd been in a bookstore. I told him how great it would be to publish a book at some point. At the time, I was working two part-time jobs while trying to make inroads as a freelance writer.

Kenny pointed out to me that I'd never have time to make it as a writer if I kept working jobs that weren't related to the work I cared about. His sentiments echoed the advice Ben had given me earlier, though Kenny's were a bit scarier. Where Ben was suggesting I focus my creative work on writing (versus trying to be in a band, too), Kenny was suggesting I stop taking paid work not related to writing, to force myself to make a living from what I loved to do. As someone who grew up with no money, this wasn't easy to process.

Kenny's words stuck with me, though, and I started focusing more on freelance writing and finding ways to cover the bills that way. When Kenny died in 2012, I flew to Calgary and gave the eulogy at his funeral. Part of what I talked about was his advice to think about time, and how we don't have endless amounts of it. It was revelatory to me at a time when I needed a revelatory moment.

Recently, I found a note that Kenny had written to my son Henry on his first birthday. The note reminded me that time is limited, and that if he hadn't inspired me to take a risk, I'd

*Stosuy, Brandon, "Visual artist Brandon Breaux on staying positive and inspired," The Creative Independent, August 9, 2018.

likely be in a very different place today. It brought me back, too, to something my mother said to me the day before she died, shortly before Henry was born: "Keep doing what you're doing." This was her concise way of telling me to prioritize what meant the most to me. It's something I think about almost every day.

We need to make time for what we love. Not making time is a form of failure, a failure to prioritize what you care about. It takes discipline, and it can be scary, but it's ultimately worth it. Here are some ways to think about time, success, and creativity:

> We've become enchanted with the idea of multitasking and lionize the multi-hyphenate creative, but juggling the demands of several projects isn't practical or beneficial depending on what's going on in your life. Set yourself up for success by being highly conscious of which projects get a yes or a no.

> You'll need to weather rejection and try multiple approaches to putting your work out there. Think about it; if success comes down to timing, why would you try *just one time*?

> Deadlines often dictate that we don't have time to make the work exactly as we wish we could. This can feel like a failure. Try looking at a deadline as a necessary starting point, or just one stage in the lifetime of an idea.

> There is no deadline for creative success. As you continue your work, old ideas can become viable. Work that went unappreciated can find an audience decades later. We don't have control of when and how our work will have impact. All we can focus on is the next step.

"Perhaps everything you do fails a little because it doesn't quite match the standard you had set, but you also succeed a little in a way you might not have foreseen. It's important to acknowledge that nothing is ever quite as we imagined—and that's the fun of it, I think."

Madeleine Dore
(Writer, interviewer, speaker, founder Extraordinary Routines)

"I think there need to be more stories about failure. Some people succeed, sure, but everyone fails . . . If you never fail, success stops being important or interesting."

Kat Gardiner
(Writer, author of *Little Wonder*)*

I fail all the time. I've gotten used to it. One thing I've learned is that adaptability is an important part of a creative life. There are ideas that exist in detours and hiccups. As my friend, the musician and academic Drew Daniel, said to me, "Sometimes you fail with regard to one objective, and by staying loose, you isolate the core of what interested you and the idea changes because you're failing to execute a badly formed idea that was a necessary starting point on the path to a better idea."

When you keep that in mind, "failure" isn't always failure, and even when it is, if you keep moving forward, you can find success in it. We can call these "happy accidents." A lot of it depends on your own relationship with the idea of failure (for instance, some people don't think failure even exists).

There's a case to be made that failure is more generative than success, particularly in the realm of creativity. Let's not forget that failure makes us more interesting and dimensional human beings; perhaps offering optimal material for making art. In this chapter, we explore how artists think of success and failure as nonbinary aspects of the creative process. What if we really, truly can't succeed without failing?

*Rachel, T. Cole, "Writer Kat Gardiner on getting your work out into the world," The Creative Independent, October 12, 2018.

When I was younger I admired big books—the ones that felt like entire worlds unto themselves—like William Gaddis's *The Recognitions*, George Elliott's *Middlemarch*, *The Brothers Karamazov* by Fyodor Dostoyevsky, Robert Musil's *The Man Without Qualities*, Marcel Proust's *In Search of Lost Time*, and later, David Foster Wallace's much-maligned *Infinite Jest*. I grew up in a place without a lot going on (or so I thought), and I liked books I could disappear into and lose my sense of surroundings. I also didn't travel much as a kid, and these books made me feel like I'd been somewhere new.

Being a novelist was an identity I'd clung to as a kid and as a teenager. I thought it was my destiny.

I walked around with a notebook in case ideas came to me. I collected sentences from my favorite books. I played with language after reading James Joyce's *Finnegans Wake*, and tried to deconstruct those sentences. I studied Virginia Woolf's prose patterns. Looking back on it, I was pretty obsessed.

So, early on in college, I tried to write a novel. My attempts seemed to go nowhere, so I shelved the book and came back to it years later. Sometimes distance works with creative projects. Here, it didn't. I tried to fill the novel with too many ideas and lost track of the plot itself. Instead of creating a world, I created a mess.

It wasn't easy to admit to myself that the book wasn't working. I remember showing a couple chapters to Jane when we first started dating. She was confused, though encouraging, because she could tell I was trying. But she was always much more impressed with the simpler kinds of writing I was doing at that time: essays, record reviews, short personal pieces. I'd thought that because that stuff came more easily, it wasn't what I should be doing. I guess I wanted to be challenged. I also think that because I grew up without a lot of money and had to work hard to get out of that situation, I assumed only things that felt difficult were worthwhile.

I did eventually come to terms with how bad the book was, and I moved on from this thing I'd spent a couple years trying to compose and simultaneously detangle. But it wasn't a waste of time. It led me to realize what I was better at, and to find a better form for my stories. It showed me that my sentences didn't need to be Henry James–long and that I didn't need to keep a thesaurus on hand. It taught me that I was good at shorter pieces about my own life and the lives of people I knew.

Lean into not just what you love, but what you can do. It can take a long time to realize that if you're good at something and it comes quickly, it's still worth doing. Conversely, it can take a long time to let go of something that isn't coming easily. Writer Daniel Alarcón describes how it felt to abandon his own novel, but how it motivated him to explore making a podcast: "It's a very sad and difficult moment of vulnerability when you realize that you've been working on a piece for however long and it sucks. But it's also at those moments of vulnerability that you're open to any and all solutions. And I was really open to the idea of tinkering with a new medium and a new genre, and learning a new language."*

Even now, my dad will occasionally ask me if I think I'm going to write a novel. Years ago, I'd feel a bit of guilt whenever he'd ask this. Nowadays, I feel a sense of peace: I've never second-guessed my decision to focus on writing, but I did come to terms with the fact that I wasn't a novelist. I figured out what I could do well and I did that instead.

*Garcia, Miriam, "Writer Daniel Alarcón on the liberation of starting over," The Creative Independent, September 18, 2018.

Right Idea, Wrong Frame

I think that so much of what we consider artistic failure is actually an issue of framing. You might be forcing your ideas into a medium or format that imposes the wrong set of limitations for your piece. Or perhaps you're attaching a label to yourself or your work that doesn't represent what you're actually making. Instead of questioning your fundamental idea, think about how it's being positioned, formatted, or contextualized. Can you see a different path for your ideas, ones that offer an escape route from failure?

"As a poet, I always want everything to be a poem, but sometimes the thing wants to be an essay, or a song, or me screaming into my pillow. It's only in the last couple of years that I've learned to follow my instincts and make a song or write an essay even if those aren't where my sharpest artistic talents lie. Everything changed when I began to take seriously the idea of myself as a vessel for thought, emotion, and communication to be channeled though. It's always more satisfying when the thing being channeled reaches others, but I came to accept that sometimes the act of release is enough. I find when I write a song or scream into the pillow, there is somehow always more room for the poem to be present with me."

J. Jennifer Espinoza
(Poet, author of *There Should Be Flowers*,
I'm Alive. It Hurts. I Love It.)

"Even though I've made moving images—mostly narrative ones—nearly half of my life, I was always reluctant to call myself a filmmaker. I do other stuff, too, but filmmaking is what I really pursued and also led to a lot of rejection. I never felt like it fit me, and also probably subconsciously, I didn't want to be saddled with all those feelings of rejection every time I said what I did. Maybe a year and a half ago, I was explaining to a friend my live cinema performance and how it was so much better than my experiences as a filmmaker, and they said something like, 'Well you're not a filmmaker, you're an artist.' That was mind-expanding to me. Mostly because I realized that yes, I primarily work with moving images, sometimes I perform the role of a screenwriter or director or filmmaker, but first and foremost, I create. And the rejection that goes along with being a filmmaker, screenwriter, and director does not live within me."

Zia Anger
(Performance artist, filmmaker)

"If you're used to playing and experimenting and making things in a nonlinear, low-stakes way, then the moments when you make something you think doesn't work feels less upsetting and dire. It's almost like failure is a muscle you have to use pretty regularly."

Heather Benjamin
(Visual artist)

The idea of "play" comes up frequently when I talk about failure with artists. We think of play as a particular moment in the creative process that's experimental and low-risk. As visual artist Laleh Khorramian puts it, "Play is when you're not really questioning. You don't ask the canon of art what happened before. You use cliché elements if you want. But it seems like playing always gets serious at some point, and that's the challenge: How to keep playing when the stakes or arenas vary."

The downside of establishing yourself as an artist on any level is the idea—and often the necessity—of delivering with consistency. "Playing was not as accessible to me once I entered a space in which I relied on my practice for everything else in my life to stay afloat," admits photographer and filmmaker Yumna Al-Arashi. "Now I am learning how to fail again, how to play, how to engage with the process of play which so often results in failure." So, how do you learn to play?

As mentioned earlier, I learned from a mentor of mine, Tony Conrad. I met him when I was a teaching assistant in the Media Studies department at SUNY Buffalo. He was in his sixties, I was in my twenties, and we hit it off immediately. We multitasked artmaking together. We put on LPs in his living room and made our own noise over it with instruments he'd built. We screened weird videos we made. I helped him write a book about music history that he never published. We tried to record a version of Dylan Thomas's radio play *Under Milk Wood*. We never completed that either.

As a kid, I thought if you didn't spend twenty years writing that Great American Novel, you weren't making art. Tony ripped that notion to shreds. Just because you didn't complete something didn't mean it wasn't a success. Every project feeds into the other, and you take small lessons from each. Through my collaborations with Tony, I learned to keep making things, avoid stagnation, and get used to the idea of tiny failures. This was during a period when I decided to focus seriously on my writing, and I think this playtime taught me to be patient and permissive with myself as a writer.

Aside from building a tolerance for failure, the obvious upside to "just playing" is the exciting breakthrough that you didn't anticipate: that happy accident. Drew Daniel, one part of the experimental electronic duo Matmos with his husband Martin, describes such an event perfectly:

> "We did a really elaborate project in the desert. It involved taking an upright piano that was busted and unfixable, wiring it inside with multiple microphones and a video camera, chaining it to a pickup truck, and then dragging it across the salt flats of the desert until it was destroyed. We did the drag, and the recordings that we got sounded dull, uninteresting, and rumbling. The project was essentially a big, labor-intensive, failed idea. . . . But the day before the desert shoot, we had laid the piano on its side, and Martin shot video of himself reaching into the piano flat on its back and stroking and rubbing its insides and manipulating some of the felt hammers. That became a really great video and sound piece that we wound up playing live for decades. So the preparatory, low-stakes, 'unimportant' moment when we were 'just playing around' turned out to be a weird success, while the highly dramatic production was a failure."

"I had wound myself up into this intolerable, self-crushing state over the ending of my novel. My friend Emily told me I had to make something just for the fuck of it. 'I'm going to make crap watercolors,' I told myself firmly. For some reason, this felt very daring and radical. I painted a dumb little robin for my pleasure only. I didn't care that it wasn't very good; it just felt fun to have a brush in my hand again, to make splashes of color like a kid; to feel the straightforward pleasure in creation."

Hermione Hoby
(Writer, critic, author of
Neon in Daylight, *Virtue*)

Playtime

What kind of space can you create for fun, low-stakes experimentation? What feels like play for you? Are you making enough time for it?

Find Your Truth Through Failure

You've decided that a project is a "failure" because it doesn't meet the standards or vision that you initially set for yourself. Now you're in an excellent position to unearth an aesthetic or an approach that is true to who you *are*, regardless of what you're striving for. It's fascinating to hear artists describe what they were aiming for and what they discovered in the process of creating what is now considered their signature work.

"My entire creative voice comes from a key foundational failure. My initial vision for my band, Thursday, was that we would be a thrashy power-violence band with a post-punk/goth vocal styling. But when we finished making the record that came to define our identity, it wasn't anything like the picture I had in my head. I spent six months depressed about this massive failure. But the failure showed me who I was: someone a lot softer and more naive than I had ever imagined. I've reconciled myself with this truer self and tried to find the ways in which I can use this empathy and sensitivity in my music."

Geoff Rickly

(Musician, songwriter, writer, vocalist of Thursday)

"I was trying to work on large pieces of paper for the first time, which felt really difficult. I was on my last sheet of paper, and I screwed up the painting. So I just started painting over it in black to 'erase' the linework. Then I started painting in negative on the black paper and it ended up being a total breakthrough for me, born totally out of a failure. Probably one of the bigger breakthroughs I've ever had, honestly."

Heather Benjamin
(Visual artist)

"I think people, myself included, generally discover their style by trying to do something they can't actually do: imitate another writer, or take on a project that doesn't suit their talents, or that in the end simply doesn't interest them. As a writer, I've come to love failure because it's some of the best and most honest feedback you can get. While success doesn't tell you much at all—it's too determined by luck—failure is yours. No one besides you cares enough to fix it. I've learned to write the way I write by trying every other method and failing at it; what remains is what distinguishes me."

Zach Baron
(Writer)

"Limits are what make style; the pattern of your dead ends is ultimately the pattern of your successes."

Zach Baron
(Writer)

Work to Failure

I train with my friend John Sharian. His workouts are difficult. When he's not a trainer, he's an actor and photographer, and he has a day job where he designs body armor for the military. We often do workouts—with a variety of different exercises and movements—where he'll tell me and my cohorts to "work to failure." You go until you can't go anymore. This directive means something different to each person. For one person, failure may mean you start to feel pain. For someone else, it may mean you work until you can literally no longer move your arms or legs, or whatever it is you're exercising. Much of it's mental. You find your own threshold.

I mentioned to John recently that I like how each person decides what failure means, and we work to that definition of it. He responded, "I like the concept because it's important to tangibly fail and have to sit with it; life failure can be too conceptual and easy to compartmentalize, so you don't get a true understanding of it."

John's workouts represent a situation where I fail in a tangible way and am forced to process what that means. For me, it's interesting to work until I can no longer move. Ideally, I push past the pain to a kind of numbness, and then I drop the weights. When I get there, it feels like a success more than a failure.

Failure Is the Goal

John's point about working to failure is interesting: Most failures are complex and due to many mitigating factors. It's hard to see your own limits—your own role in the equation—and this is valuable information. Set yourself up for failure by working on something far outside of your comfort zone. When you want to give up, push a little more. What do you notice?

_____

_____

_____

_____

_____

_____

_____

_____

_____

_____

_____

_____

_____

_____

Failure and Opportunity

"After graduating from university, I had the not-uncommon experience of finding it difficult to find work in my chosen field of journalism. I felt like a failure—I was unemployed and felt pretty disheartened that I was unable to find work while friends around me were making leaps and bounds in their newly formed careers. I knew that I enjoyed interviewing and meeting interesting people and needed to find a way to bring those experiences into my life, even if no one was offering to pay me. So I chipped away at starting a side project, Extraordinary Routines, in 2014, and I've been adding interviews, life experiments, and musings to the site ever since. In time, the personal project helped me land a job as staff writer and helped shape my freelance career. It was the basis for an event series, a podcast, and most recently, a book deal. Not to mention countless friendships, insights, and new ways of thinking about how to live creatively. So I'd say now that if you can't find the job you want, create it—that doesn't have to be a grand commitment, even the smallest steps can lead you in an entirely new direction in time."

Madeleine Dore
(Writer, interviewer, speaker,
founder of Extraordinary Routines)

Never Mind the Gatekeepers

Sometimes losing a job or failing to make it past the gatekeepers of your field is the spark you need to start your own project. It may not be the ideal vision you had, but flexibility goes a long way here, and you can still be optimistic and proud with a different path. What can you create on your own?

_____

_____

_____

_____

_____

_____

_____

_____

_____

_____

_____

_____

_____

_____

_____

_____

_____

What DIY Projects Have You Launched to Get Around Gatekeepers?

"I began my literary magazine, *Witch Craft Magazine*, with the hopes of publishing writers whose work subverted the kind of fiction I was reading in major magazines. I also have gone the route of submitting my more experimental work to smaller, but cooler, presses who aren't afraid to take risks."

Elle Nash
(Writer, critic, author of *Animals Eat Each Other* and *Nudes*, founder of *Witch Craft Magazine*)

"A few bands that I've been in have invented fake booking agents and created email accounts for them for the purpose of negotiating show bookings. Promoters are a lot more likely to respond to people working in the industry than they are to respond to artists!"

Felix Walworth
(Musician, producer, photographer, performs as Told Slant)

"When I started doing stand-up, it was harder to get booked on 'cool' shows, so my friends and I started running our own show, and we booked other comics our age. We had the freedom to try stuff out because the audiences were smaller. I have repeated this formula many times."

Josh Fadem
(Actor/comedian, *30 Rock*, *Better Call Saul*, *Twin Peaks*)

"I remember how difficult I found it to get my work accepted for group shows, so I reached out to a few friends who were in the same place as I was at the time, and we came up with our own art collective. We only had time for a couple of shows, but it made us all so proud and showed us how capable and strong we could be if we did things ourselves, together."

Noelia Towers
(Visual artist)

Failure and Opportunity

Rejecting the Success/Failure Binary

I asked artists about their failures, and an overwhelming number responded that they take issue with the word "failure" itself; that it erases context and implies standards that aren't relevant in the first place. For example, musician and curator Taja Cheek says, "I'm trying to grow beyond the idea of 'excellence' all together, which also means that I have to move beyond the idea of 'failure.' When activists urge us to embrace more expansive definitions of gender and demand the abolition of prisons regardless of innocence and guilt, I feel inspired in my own small way to imagine a new world with other dissolved binaries. In imagining this new world, I wonder if 'good' and 'bad' become completely inept descriptors, along with 'success' and 'failure.' Could we be better served by a more nuanced conversation around what things are—how they operate and why—rather than a preoccupation with 'taste' and 'goodness' which is not super specific or helpful, and is ultimately completely subjective?"

We live within systems that function around ideas of success and failure: a school system, a legal system, an economic system. Our creative work simply cannot live and die within the rules of these systems. Naama Tsabar, an installation and performance artist, asks the necessary questions: "What is failure? Who sets the standards? And why don't I fit within these standards? And what can I do with that? You see it a lot in dance today, for example, in choreography where this idea of the movement, the body, this rigid idea of a dancer has been completely broken by this idea of going outside of the order, and reclaiming it as you do so."*

* Stosuy, Brandon, "Naama Tsabar on taking control of your process," The Creative Independent, April 4, 2017.

Choreographer Sigrid Lauren, one half of the performance duo FlucT, picks up this thread about the evolution of dance and relates it to an evolution in pedagogy, where the limitations of each performer define the development of a piece: "I'm reading this book called *The Queer Art of Failure*. It talks about how new ideas aren't conceived by following a straight-lined path, doing exactly what the teacher tells you. Everybody is so different, and a straight line won't work for all and won't produce a new wiggly line. It is something that's been really prevalent for our practice. We're not worrying about, 'Oh man, I can't do this one kick so high.' It's like, 'OK, well then you kick your leg into my hand, I'll throw it that high and then I'll catch your neck so you don't fall.'"**

Poet J. Jennifer Espinoza echoes all of these ideas: "A large portion of what I write is about failing to perform gender in an expected way. Because this is such a focus in my work, I've learned to embrace failure as a form of insight and potential. It's easy to become less fearful of failure when you find yourself failing at something you don't believe in or desire." Clearly, one path to overcoming a fear of failure is to reject the very premise and standards of success. Failure then becomes your guiding principle, rather than something to avoid.

Think about some of the rules that you've been operating within, especially with regard to your creative work. Which rules define your failures? What would it look like if you followed your failures, instead of following the rules?

** Stosuy, Brandon, "Performance duo FlucT on using your body to tell stories," The Creative Independent, September 10, 2018.

Failure Is a Cultural Construct

In a society that is dominantly defined by capitalism and individualism, it's easy to see why failure is perceived as individual responsibility, and conversely, that success is due to an individual's talent and hard work. Taking full responsibility for your failures and successes is something that we've been trained to do under a larger cultural narrative (one that arguably undervalues the collective structures that make opportunities possible to begin with).

"There's this great book, *Born Losers,* that sketches out the relationship between American notions of failure and the evolution of capitalism. America sees wealth and prosperity as proof of one's moral standing. And the reverse is true, too; it's your fault if you can't provide for yourself. It made me wonder what failure looks like outside of capitalism? What if our lives weren't calibrated to questions of winning and losing? Would the question of failure then illuminate the obligations we have to one another that aren't about profit and loss?"

Hua Hsu

(*The New Yorker* staff writer, professor, author of *A Floating Chinaman: Fantasy and Failure Across the Pacific*)

"In the modern era of 'self as brand,' we are encouraged to be perfectionists and to take a kind of masochistic pleasure in being tough on ourselves, or 'our own worst critic.' But that can often come from a weirdly myopic understanding of what an artist is, the lone hero mythos that separates this isolated individual from the surrounding mesh of institutions, scenes, supporting figures, mentors, fans, friends, etc. If you look at many artists, they have a constellation around them that lifts them up, tells them awkward truths about what's working and what could be worked on more, that nurtures and supports. Frankly, some societies also support artmaking and creative work directly and financially in ways that other societies and social orders do not. It's not all about the individual as the unit of measure."

Drew Daniel
(Musician, writer, professor,
Soft Pink Truth, Matmos)

Five Definitions of Success

Do you ever really know if you have a success on your hands? Here are five thoughts about success that highlight what a slippery and contradictory concept it is:

1. A successful formula may start to feel like a failure.

"I feel like I've been really stuck in just following a linear trajectory of making the kind of work that is well-received and 'works for me,' and haven't made enough time for play and experimentation, and have therefore kind of fallen out of practice of failing gracefully."

Heather Benjamin
(Visual artist)

2. Success (and failure) are not intrinsic to the work itself.

"There are pieces I've worked incredibly hard at and believed in totally that have come out and gone almost entirely unremarked upon; there are other pieces that I have felt like I never totally solved that people seemed to love. Your definition of failure and someone else's are rarely the same. I find this liberating. You start to learn to separate the reception of the thing from the thing itself."

Zach Baron
(Writer)

3. Success (and failure) are simultaneously present in all work.

"I think my work is all about failure: our failure to see ourselves, our failure to properly see others. It's easier to forgive my characters for this, and to love them through it, than to do the same for myself. I recently read *Crime and Punishment* for the first time. It's arguably not that good! A great novel that's also not that good. This exhilarated me."

Hermione Hoby

(Writer, critic, author of *Neon in Daylight, Virtue*)

4. Success might be something only you can see.

"I've definitely written poems that I felt were successful, only to have the response be tepid. In those moments, I remind myself that sometimes it's OK for the poem to be a conversation with myself, and I've learned to look for elements that separate poems I want to share with others from poems that are perhaps there for me and only me to learn something from."

J. Jennifer Espinoza

(Poet, author of *There Should Be Flowers,*
I'm Alive. It Hurts. I Love It.)

5. Success is an outcome that you can't possibly see.

"I feel successful when I have shown myself something that I have imagined but never seen before. I only get to know myself when I am left feeling strange or uncomfortable in what I have made. The concrete material end of the creation of an artwork should leave one questioning, rather than providing some sort of affirmation. The affirmation would be a cue to stop. Mission accomplished."

Matthew Day Jackson

(Visual artist)

Conclusion

"More recently than I would like to admit, I wrote a bad novel. The day I realized this—that it was a failure—was actually an excellent day; I felt at peace because I could finally start fresh and try again, knowing what I now knew."

Zach Baron
(Writer)

One gift of failure that we haven't touched on—and one that is appropriate for the conclusion of a book—is closure. If nothing else, failure is a signal that it's time to move on from a particular project, mindset, or goal. It's time to make space for something new.

Madeleine Dore describes a "failure signal," that came to her in the form of burnout after running an event series called Side Project Sessions for a few years. She designed the series to help people carve out time for their side projects. Ironically, Madeleine found its success depleting: "If I were to follow the thread to find the cause for burnout, I'd find failure—failure to ask for help, failure to determine the right model to grow, failure to define my own metrics of success for the project, failure to see that just because you created something doesn't mean you're the best person to run it."

Madeleine ended the Side Project Sessions and instead created a digital workbook for sharing the methodology behind the events. She reframed "failure" as a "learning to let go," and as a result, made room for new opportunities (including getting a book deal). "So I believe that's how we continue to find momentum in our work and in our lives. The more things you try, the more ease you develop in letting go when it's not working, the more chance you have at succeeding at something else."

When I was a kid, I thought that if I reached a specific goal—for instance, publishing a review in the *Village Voice* or interviewing a punk band I admired—it would mean I'd "made it." (Once, sitting in a tour bus in Trenton, New Jersey, with the Southern California pop punk group the Descendents I thought, "This is it.") As I got older and I hit these and other modest goals, I realized I'd been wrong: Until we die, we never reach a finish line. When one project ends, another is usually waiting, and we have to figure out (all over again) how to get started.

This isn't meant to be discouraging. Personally, I've found it exciting to realize I have more than one idea, that goals continually shift, and that I can return to things I'd skipped or abandoned or simply forgotten about at a later time. Ideas don't die just because you didn't have the time or angle when they first came to you. There's always something around the corner, and the trick is to keep moving. Here are some ways to practice the art of letting go:

> Let go of the formats or labels that you are attaching to your ideas. What does your work really want to be?

> Let go of the pressure to find linear, self-engineered solutions. When you are at an impasse, it's time to play and create potential for happy accidents.

> Let go of the need for permission to create. If you're cut off by gatekeepers, do what you can with your own resources.

> Let go of the rules that define what "fails" and what "succeeds." Exposing the limitations and often unfair constructs at the foundation of these rules is the very definition of creativity.

Acknowledgments

I want to thank everyone who contributed to *How to Fail Successfully*. It's difficult talking about failure, and I was impressed by how willing people were to share their experiences. A special nod goes to the musicians I manage: Anna, Aoife, Indigo, Katie, Lydia, Meg, and ṠB, thanks a ton. Playing a role in what you do is inspiring and it makes my life better.

I'd also like to thank my editor, Karrie Witkin. I've learned so much about myself and my process by seeing how she refines, deepens, corrals, and connects. Thanks, too, to my agent, Chad Luibl, whose kindness and enthusiasm has been . . . unfailing.

Thanks so much to the incredible team at Abrams, especially Jessica Focht, Samantha Weiner, and Elizabeth Broussard. Also, thank you to Kristian Henson and Jenice Kim for the beautiful illustrations and design.

One of the upsides of quarantine this past year is doing so much with my family—hikes, cooking projects, football in the park, dance parties—and wanting even more time with them. Henry and Jake, I'm so proud of you (even when you're making fun of my terrible dancing). Speaking of terrible dancers: If my father hadn't been open to my ideas as a kid, I may not have had as many creative failures, and wouldn't have gotten to where I am now.

When my wife, Jane, and I first met, I told her I could fix her car. She realized I had no idea what I was doing the second I asked her how to open the hood. For the past twenty years, she's been there when I've failed and helped me keep going. It's heartening to reflect on the success of our love for each other. But honestly, I still wouldn't be able to fix that car.